1

Matthew 5-7

Storm Proof

Blessed

(Matthew 5:1-12)

1. Take a moment and pray. Ask the Lord to prepare your heart for all He wants to say through this study. Ask Him to open your eyes so you can truly behold these great truths He so graciously preserved in His Word. Ask Him to help you approach familiar verses with a fresh perspective. Thank Him that His Word is alive and able to instruct, comfort, reveal and enlighten.

2. Where was Jesus and who was around him when he was giving this teaching?

_____

_____

_____

_____

3. What does "Blessed" mean in Matt 5:3-11? This is a link to its Greek origin. Feel free to select the Vine's Expository Dictionary on the site. https://www.blueletterbible.org/lang/lexicon/lexicon.cfm?Strongs=G3107&t=KJV . What does this tell us about the kind of lives these teachings are intended to give us?

_____

_____

_____

_____

_____

4. What do these verses teach us about being poor in spirit?

     a. Isaiah 57:15-16_____

_____

_____

_____

     b. Isaiah 66:2_____

_____

_____

_____

5. What is promised to those who mourn?

_____

6. Record what 2 Corinthians 1:3-4 says about who comforts us, when we are comforted and what God wants us to do with the comfort?

_____

_____

_____

_____

_____

_____

_____

_____

7. What kind of people will find themselves being filled and not empty according to Matt. 5:6?

_____

_____

8. Read Isaiah 55:1-2. What is the Lord saying about what we really hunger and thirst for?

_____

_____

_____

9. How has God been merciful to you?

_____

_____

_____

_____

10. Read James 2:13. What do we learn is more powerful than judgment?_____

11. What might make it difficult to show mercy to another? What could we do to cultivate merciful responses to those who may fall short in some way? _____

_____

_____

_____

_____

12. What does Proverbs 11:17 say about the merciful person?_____

_____

> *Blessed are the pure in heart:*
>
> *for they shall see God.*
>
> Matthew 5:8

13. Why do you believe having a pure heart is essential for recognizing God in our lives? Support with scripture if you can.

_____

_____

_____

_____

_____

14. What does Psalm 34:12-14 say will be a benefit of being someone who seeks to bring peace in relationships? _____

_____

_____

15. What should be our response when we have people come against us for our walk with the Lord according to Matthew 5:11-12? Why does Jesus say we should respond this way?

_____

_____

_____

_____

_____

16. Take a moment to pray for all the attributes the Lord says will make us blessed. Ask Him to make you like this and then thank Him for the possible results when you conduct yourself in this manner.

Blessed are the poor in spirit, For theirs is the kingdom of heaven.

Blessed are those who mourn, For they shall be comforted.

Blessed are the meek, For they shall inherit the earth.

Blessed are those who hunger and thirst for righteousness, For they shall be filled.

Blessed are the merciful, For they shall obtain mercy.

Blessed are the pure in heart, For they shall see God.

Blessed are the peacemakers, For they shall be called sons of God.

Blessed are those who are persecuted for righteousness' sake,

For theirs is the kingdom of heaven.

Blessed are you when they revile and persecute you, and say all kinds of evil against you falsely for My sake.

Great

(Matthew 5:13-20)

1. What does Jesus say His followers are like in Matt 5:13?_____

2. Research 'salt' and list some of its uses.

_____

_____

_____

_____

_____

3. What can we learn about how the Lord wants to affect this world by understanding the uses and properties of salt?

_____

_____

_____

_____

_____

4. What kind of lamps did people use at the time of Jesus?_____

_____

_____

> *You are the light of the world.*
>
> *(Matt 5:14)*

5. Why does the Lord say a lamp is put on a lampstand?_____

_____

6. In what ways could we be guilty of putting our lights under baskets?_____

_____

_____

_____

_____

7. Look at the following verses about light(s) and record your thoughts.

     a. 1 Thess. 5:5_____

_____

_____

     b. Eph. 5:8_____

_____

_____

c. Acts 13:47_____

_____

_____

d. Phil 2:14-16_____

_____

_____

_____

_____

8. Who should be getting the glory for good works that we do? _____

_____

9. How might we avoid getting the credit for good works and bring Him glory?

_____

_____

_____

_____

10. How did the Lord say His mission worked with the law and the prophets?

_____

_____

_____

_____

11. What do we learn about God's written Word in Matt 5:18? _____

_____

_____

12. Read Isaiah 40:8. What do we learn about God's Word?_____

_____

_____

13. How can knowing the reliability and steadfast endurance of the Word of God help us put our lights on the lampstand?

_____

_____

_____

_____

14. Who does Jesus say will be called great in the kingdom of heaven?_____

_____

_____

15. What does Jesus say in Matt 5:20?

_____

_____

_____

16. How does Romans 9:31-32 explain the righteousness the Jews found their confidence in?_____

_____

_____

_____

_____

_____

You Have Heard

(Matthew 5:21-28)

1. What does Jesus say we have heard in Matthew 5:21? _____

_____

2. What does He say in response to what they had heard? _____

_____

3. Describe some scenarios where anger would be intertwined with murder? _____

_____

_____

_____

_____

_____

4. What do these verses say about anger?

    a. Psalm 37:8 _____

_____

_____

_____

    b. Proverbs 29:22 _____

_____

_____

_____

5. What is the first murder we read about in the bible. Look at Genesis 4:4-8. Record your observations in this tragedy based on what Jesus says in Matthew 5:22. _____

_____
_____
_____
_____

6. What can we do to avoid being angry with others?_____

_____
_____
_____

7. How can calling others names sever relationships and make it difficult to restore such relationships?_____

_____
_____
_____

8. Our relationship with God is directly linked to our relationships with others. What can we learn about ourselves if we can confidently approach God, knowing we have sinned against another and haven't tried to make it right?_____

_____
_____
_____
_____
_____
_____

9. What does the Lord want us to do after we are reconciled to a person?_____

_____

10. What do these verses say about reconciling with people?

     a. Matthew 18:15 _____

_____

     b. Romans 12:18 _____

_____

11. Seeing where we might have wronged someone before it escalates, will help us avoid unnecessary painful consequences. How might we be open to seeing where we might have wronged someone?_____

_____

_____

_____

_____

_____

12. What did Jesus say they had heard in verse 27? _____

_____

13. What does Jesus say in verse 28?

_____

_____

14. Jesus deals with the mind and eyes before the action. If a man already intends to pursue a woman outside of the marriage covenant, he is already on the road to commit it. His heart and mind are the starting points for the action. How could a person avoid adultery by first taking heed to their eyes and mind?_____

_____

_____

_____

_____

_____

15. Read Genesis 34:1-2. How did the sexual sin begin?_____

_____

16. Look at 2 Samuel 11:2-4. How did the eyes contribute to sexual sin?_____

_____

_____

17. Pray for your church family. Pray for those who struggle with anger. Pray for those who might be looking to commit adultery with someone to confess to an adulteress heart. Pray for the hearts of your church family to be upright in the eyes of the Lord, preventing sin that could be birthed from anger or lust.

'Yes' and 'No'

(Matthew 5:29-37)

1. What does Jesus say the right hand and the right eye could cause us to do in Matthew 5:29-30?_____

2. What do we learn from Jesus about taking extreme measures to keep us from sin?

_____

_____

3. Read Romans 6:11-12. As followers of Jesus what is to be our relationship to sin?_____

_____

_____

4. Consider different sinful patterns. Name a pattern and then give some practical measures people might take to break these patterns._____

_____

_____

_____

_____

_____

_____

_____

_____

_____

5. Looking at Matthew 5:31-32, what does Jesus say about divorce and remarriage?

_____

_____

_____

_____

_____

_____

6. What do we read about divorce in Malachi 2:16?_____

_____

7. What are some negative ramifications people may experience from divorce?_____

_____

_____

_____

_____

_____

_____

8. What do we learn in 1 Cor 7:10-11?

_____

_____

_____

9. What does 1 Cor 7:12-13 say about believers that are married to unbelievers?_____

_____

_____

_____

10. What do we learn in 1 Cor 7:15?_____

_____

_____

11. Read Mark 10:2-5. What does Jesus say is often the reason for perceived irreconcilable difference? _____

_____

12. Jesus takes a stand on speaking oaths in Matthew 5:33-36. Why does He say to not swear by 'heaven'?_____

_____

13. Why does He say we shouldn't swear by 'the earth'?_____

_____

14. Why are we not supposed to swear by 'Jerusalem'?_____

_____

15. Why are we not to swear by 'our heads'?

_____

_____

16. What does Jesus say in Matthew 5:37?

_____

_____

_____

_____

_____

_____

19

17. When we add to our words by swearing upon something, Jesus tells us where these additives come from. Where do these additional words come from?_____

_____

18. How might we be more careful with being truthful in ALL we say?_____

_____

_____

19. What benefits would we find if we speak the truth at all times?_____

_____

_____

20. How can the 'yes' and 'no' instruction help us stay committed in marriage, avoid adultery and not give in to temptation?_____

_____

_____

_____

_____

But I Say

(Matthew 5:38-48)

1. What does Jesus say to do in Matthew 5:39? Try to read a few different versions of the bible and summarize here._____

_____

_____

_____

2. Record what we learn in these verses.

    a. 1 Thessalonians 5:15_____

    _____

    b. 1 Peter 3:9_____

    _____

    _____

    c. Romans 12:17-19_____

    _____

    _____

    _____

3. Read 1 Peter 2:19-23.

    a. Jot down what we learn in these verses about attitude and responses. _____

    _____

    _____

b. What did Jesus do when He was treated unfairly?_____

_____

_____

c. How can seeing the Lord as our advocate help us respond better when we are mistreated?_____

_____

_____

4. Matthew 5:40 addresses offenses involving things we own. What do the following verses teach us about our possessions?

a. Proverbs 3:9 _____

_____

_____

b. Colossians 3:2 _____

_____

_____

c. Proverbs 13:7_____

_____

_____

d. 1 Timothy 6:17_____

_____

_____

Heb 10:34-35

...joyfully accepted the plundering of your goods, knowing that you have a better and an enduring possession for yourselves in heaven.

5. Matthew 5:41 deals with exerting energy and taking time on the behalf of someone else. Why would it be difficult to do this for someone who expects you to be this way?_____

_____

_____

_____

6. How might we make ourselves ready to 'go the extra mile' on behalf of someone else?

_____

_____

_____

7. How can going beyond another's expectation reflect the beauty of our Lord?

_____

_____

_____

_____

8. Jesus deals with our money in Matthew 5:42. How might financially helping others guard our hearts from the love of money?_____

_____

_____

_____

9. Look at Proverbs 3:27-28. What are we told in these verses? _____

_____

_____

_____

10. Jesus tells His listeners that they have heard to love your neighbor and hate your enemy. What does Leviticus 19:18 say? What does it say about your enemy?_____

_____

_____

11. Look at Matthew 5:44. What does Jesus say we should do to...

    a. ...our enemies?_____

    _____

    b. ...those who curse us?_____

    _____

    c. ...those who hate us?_____

    _____

    d. ...those who spitefully use us and
       persecute us?_____

    _____

12. Why does the Lord tell us to do these things according to Matthew 5:45?_____

_____

_____

_____

_____

13. Jesus points out what we naturally do in Matthew 5:46-47. What do all humans naturally do in relationships?_____

_____

_____

14. Who does Matthew 5:48 tell us we will be like if we order our conduct according to Matthew 5:38-48?_____

_____

15. In what ways has your Father in heaven gone the extra mile for you?_____

_____

_____

_____

_____

_____

_____

Luke 6:35-36

But love your enemies, do good, and lend, hoping for nothing in return; and your reward will be great, and you will be sons of the Most High. For He is kind to the unthankful and evil.

But You

(Matthew 6:1-8)

Read Matthew 6:1-4. Answer the following questions.

1. What does verse 1 say shouldn't be our motivation when we do charitable deeds?

_____

_____

_____

2. Who is to be the One we are concerned about pleasing when doing good deeds?_____

_____

3. What will the Lord do for us when we do our charitable deeds with the least amount of attentions as possible?_____

_____

4. Many good deeds will be seen by others. Does this necessarily mean they are being done in order *to be seen* by others? Explain. _____

_____

_____

_____

_____

_____

_____

_____

5. Jesus teaches us a bit about prayer in Matthew 6:5-8. What are some of the things He says about prayer in these verses?

_____

_____

_____

_____

_____

_____

_____

_____

_____

_____

6. What was the reason hypocrites loved to pray standing the synagogues?_____

_____

7. Look at Galatians 1:10. What does Paul explain in this verse?_____

_____

_____

8. Read what Jesus warned his disciples about in Luke 20:45-47. What did He say about the scribes and their prayers?_____

_____

_____

_____

_____

9. How could you obey Jesus in finding a private place to pray to your Father?

_____

_____

_____

_____

10. We know group prayer and public prayer is taught and exemplified in the scriptures. Why would personal, private prayer be something the Father greatly delights in?_____

_____

_____

_____

11. What do we learn about the quantity of words used in prayer in Matthew 6:7?

_____

_____

12. Jesus tells us why we don't need to use a quantity of words in Matthew 6:8. What is this reason?_____

_____

15. What does Psalm 139:3-4 reveal about God's familiarity with us?_____

_____

_____

_____

In This Manner

(Matthew 6:9-13)

1. What possessive pronoun is before 'Father' in this prayer?_____

2. How could using this possessive pronoun impact our perspective on the Father/child relationship God has with His people?

_____

_____

_____

3. How could starting our prayers acknowledging how holy God is, impact the way we pray?

_____

_____

4. Find a few verses talking about God's holiness. Write them here and record your thoughts about them?_____

_____

_____

_____

_____

_____

_____

_____

_____

5. Whose 'will' and 'kingdom' is to be considered in our prayers? What does this mean to you?_____

_____

_____

_____

_____

_____

6. What could be some indicators that our prayers might be centered more on our own wills or kingdoms?_____

_____

_____

_____

7. What does Matthew 6:11 say about when we should expect to be given what we need?

_____

8. Read Proverbs 30:8. How does this prayer mirror Matthew 6:11?_____

_____

_____

_____

9. Look at Matthew 6:12. What is Jesus asking us to deal with when we pray to our Father?

_____

10. What two relationships is the Lord asking us to deal with in prayer in Matthew 6:12?

_____

11.   What does Mark 11:25-26 record Jesus saying in regards to the forgiveness we give others and the forgiveness we receive from God?

_____

_____

_____

_____

12. What does Jesus say we should pray according to Matthew 6:13? How can this produce a spiritual alertness when we are facing our days?_____

_____

_____

_____

13. How does Jesus say we should end our prayers according to Matthew 6:13?

_____

_____

_____

14. Why would starting out with God's kingdom and ending with His kingdom help us pray in the way the Lord wants us to?_____

_____

_____

_____

_____

15. Take a moment and pray Matthew 6:9-13.

When You

(Matthew 6:14-20)

1. Matthew 6:14 addresses the seriousness of extending forgiveness to others. What could make it difficult to forgive someone?

_____
_____
_____

2. God is the ultimate example of someone who forgives. Look at the following verses and record what we learn about our God.

a. Psalm 99:8_____

_____
_____

b. Psalm 103:2-4_____

_____
_____

c. John 8:11_____

_____
_____

d. Jeremiah 33:8_____

_____
_____

e. Nehemiah 9:17_____

_____
_____

32

3. In Matthew 6:16 we read why the hypocrites do certain things when they are fasting. Why do they do this?_____
_____

4. What is the reward Jesus is referring to in Matthew 6:16?_____
_____

5. What does Jesus tell his disciples to do when fasting? (Matthew 6:17-18)

_____
_____
_____
_____
_____

6. How can we minimize the attention we could get when we fast?_____
_____
_____
_____

7. Why do you believe Jesus emphasizes doing things in a way which only our heavenly Father sees?_____
_____
_____
_____
_____

Luke 16:15

...For what is highly esteemed among men is an abomination in the sight of God.

8. Read Matthew 23:5-7. Record what Jesus was warning His followers about in these verses?

_____

_____

_____

_____

9. Why would a believer desire the attention of others when fasting?_____

_____

_____

_____

10.   What can happen to earthly treasures according to Matthew 6:19?_____

_____

_____

11. Where should our treasures be?_____

_____

12. List some heavenly treasures. Give scripture references to support your thoughts._____

_____

_____

_____

_____

No One

(Matthew 6:21-26)

1. As we read Matthew 6:21, what do we learn about what we treasure and where our hearts are?_____

_____

_____

2. Why do you suppose our treasures are associated with the affections of our hearts?

_____

_____

_____

_____

_____

3. Look at Colossians 3:1-2. What does the Lord tell us about our hearts and treasures?

_____

_____

_____

_____

4. What sort of things could believers treasure that might lure away their affection for the things which are from above?

_____

_____

_____

_____

35

5. What does Matthew 6:22-23 say about our 'eyes' and our beings?_____

_____

_____

_____

_____

_____

6. How can a believer better guard what we see or take in?_____

_____

_____

_____

6. How does what you take in, affect you? _____

_____

7. Describe a time you were adversely affected by something you saw or heard._____

_____

_____

_____

_____

8. Describe a time you were positively affected by something you saw or heard.

_____

_____

_____

_____

_____

_____

9. What does Matthew 6:24 say about being able to serve more than one master?_____

_____

_____

10. What other 'masters' could compete for lordship in a believer's life?_____

_____

11. What two masters does James 4:4 refer to? What does this verse explain?_____

_____

_____

_____

12. What does the Lord say in Matthew 6:25?

_____

_____

_____

_____

_____

13. Why would worrying about eating, drinking or clothing contribute to serving money?

_____

_____

_____

_____

_____

_____

_____

14. Where does the Lord want us to look to according to Matthew 6:26?_____

_____

_____.

15. What can we learn from the birds?

_____

_____

_____

_____

_____

Why Worry?

(Matthew 6:27-34)

1. What does Jesus ask in Matthew 6:27?

_____

_____

2. Look at Philippians 4:6-7. What are we told to do instead of worrying?

_____

3. Why would 'giving thanks' in the midst of our petitions contribute to peace?

_____

_____

_____

_____

4. What should we learn from the flowers about our concern for what we will wear?

_____

_____

_____

_____

_____

_____

_____

_____

5. Jesus tells us some worries we shouldn't have in Matthew 6:31. What are they?

_____

_____

_____

6. In Matthew 6:32, our Lord explains who is primarily concerned with these things. Who does He refer to? _____

7. In Ephesians 4:17 believers are told to no longer conduct themselves as what?

_____

8. What do these verses speak to us about concerning this world and God's kingdom?

    a. Matthew 13:22_____

    _____

    _____

    b. John 18:36_____

    _____

    _____

    c. 1 Timothy 6:7_____

    _____

    _____

    d. John 15:19_____

    _____

    _____

9. "...your heavenly Father knows that you need all these things." (Matt 6:32) What are the things He knows we need?_____

_____

10. What are believers supposed to seek according to Matthew 6:33?_____

_____

_____

11. What does Jesus tell us about the worries we have about things we are not yet facing?

_____

_____

_____

_____

_____

12. Trust is often the cure for worry. What do these verses say about trust?

    a. Psalm 18:2_____

       _____

       _____

    b. Psalm 37:3_____

       _____

       _____

    C. Psalm 118:8_____

       _____

       _____

       _____

FOCUS

(Matthew 7:1-8)

1. How could we propagate an atmosphere of criticism in our relationships?_____

_____

_____

_____

_____

2. What can we do to redirect our thoughts from analysis and judgements in relationships?

_____

_____

_____

_____

_____

3. Why might it be easier to see certain flaws more than others in those around us?_____

_____

_____

_____

4. What does Jesus say will happen to us when we focus on something He is asking us to get rid of and successfully remove it from our lives?

_____

_____

_____

_____

5. How can guarding things that are truly valuable protect us from falling apart when storms may hit our lives?_____

_____

_____

_____

_____

6. What do the following verses teach us about what we should value?

    a. Psalm 119:127_____

       _____

    b. Proverbs 3:13-15_____

       _____

    c. Proverbs 8:10_____

       _____

    d. Proverbs 8:18-19_____

       _____

7. How can we increase our ability to discern when a relationship or pursuit might not be worthy of our time, gifts or attention?

_____

_____

_____

_____

_____

8. What did Jesus say would happen to us after the things we value are trampled under their feet?_____
_____
_____

9. How might we be careful to not trample things that are valuable to others under OUR feet?

_____
_____
_____
_____
_____

10. What three things does Jesus tell us to do in Matthew 7:7-8?_____
_____

11. What three results will occur if we obey His commands in this verse?_____
_____

ASK
and ye shall receive

SEEK
and ye shall find

KNOCK
and it shall be opened

12. How would a believer obey these commands?_____

_____
_____
_____
_____

13. Have you ever found yourself not finding, receiving or having doors opened and concluded you weren't REALLY asking, seeking and knocking? Explain._____

_____
_____
_____
_____

14. Read James 4:3. What do we learn about 'asking' and 'receiving' in this text?_____

_____
_____

15. What can we do to purify our prayer life? How can we be sensitive to any ongoing sin in our lives that may hinder it or worldly agendas mixed in with our requests?_____

_____
_____
_____
_____
_____
_____

Much More

(Matthew 7:9-11)

1. To what relationship does the Lord liken our relationship with God in these verses?

_____

2. What items is the son asking for in these verses?_____

_____

3. What does Jesus say an earthly father would not give their child in response to these requests?

_____

_____

4. What does Jesus say an earthly father knows how to do in Matthew 7:11?_____

_____

5. Look at Genesis 1:27. Whose image are we made in?_____

6. What do we learn about our Heavenly Father by seeing this conclusion about earthly parents? .

_____

_____

_____

_____

_____

_____

7. Why would a person with a poor relationship with their earthly father might have a hard time trusting their Heavenly Father?_____

_____

_____

_____

_____

8. What advice could you give someone in bringing them to a place of knowing and trusting God as their Heavenly Father?

_____

_____

_____

_____

_____

_____

_____

9. How can our understanding of who our Heavenly Father impact our understanding of prayer and answers to prayer?_____

_____

_____

_____

10. Parents are the first representation of our heavenly father to children. How can a parent better represent God to their offspring?_____

_____

_____

_____

_____

11. Does Jesus say that earthly parents WILL give the child the specific item that child requested?

_____

12. What does this teach us about the prayers and answers we may experience?

_____

_____

_____

_____

13. Consider prayers you have made in the past that were not answered according to your particular ideas. Were there any denied or fulfilled in a different way than requested, that you see was God's great wisdom and love for you? Explain._____

_____

_____

_____

_____

_____

_____

_____

14. Pause now and pray. Thank God for being a Good, Good, Father. Let Him know you trust Him to answer according to wisdom and knowledge you do not have. Rest in His faithful love towards you. Thank Him for being YOUR Father in Heaven.

As You Want

(Matthew 7:12-14)

1. How does the Lord sum up the Law and Prophets in Matthew 7:12?_____

_____

_____

2. How do you like to be treated by people?

_____

_____

_____

_____

_____

3. What do you want someone to do to you if you sin against them? Give your answer in concrete examples you would want to see come forth from the way they treat you.

_____

_____

_____

_____

_____

4. What if you did it intentionally? _____

_____

_____

_____

5. What kind of response do you want from people as you are seeking to overcome a pattern of behavior that might be difficult for others to put up with?_____

_____

_____

_____

_____

6. How do you want to be treated when you wound someone and aren't aware that you did?

_____

_____

_____

_____

_____

7. Look back over your previous answers and consider people in your life that have done any of these things to you. Have you treated them as you want others to treat you? Explain. _____

_____

_____

_____

_____

_____

8. How can we be more aware of any double standards in our lives as far as our expectations on others versus the standards we hold to our own actions?_____

_____

_____

_____

_____

_____

9. Read Romans 13:8-10. Explain how love fulfills the Law. _____

_____

_____

_____

_____

10. Contrast the two entrances Jesus refers to in Matthew 7:13-14._____

_____

_____

_____

_____

11. What does John 14:6 say about the way to the Father? Explain._____

_____

_____

_____

_____

_____

12. What is His command to us regarding the 'narrow gate'?_____

_____

13. Contrast the numbers of people taking the two choices._____

_____

14. Where does the narrow gate lead?

_____

15. Where does the wide gate lead?

_____

16. Pray for those who have yet to have entered in this narrow gate. Pray for them to recognize it and take the necessary steps to enter it.

Beware

(Matthew 7:15-20)

1. What does the Lord tell us to be aware of in Matthew 7:15?_____

2. Read 1 John 4:1. What are we told in this text?

_____

_____

_____

3. Why would succumbing to false prophets in our lives compromise the structure of our lives?

_____

_____

_____

4. What does the Lord tell us in Matthew 7:16 to better evaluate if someone is a false prophet?

_____

_____

_____

_____

5. What do these verses say about fruit?

   a. John 15:2_____

   _____

   _____

b. John 15:8_____

_____

_____

c. Luke 3:9_____

_____

_____

6. What do these verses say about false teachers/prophets?

a. Matthew 24:24_____

_____

_____

b. 2 Peter 2:1-3_____

_____

_____

_____

_____

_____

_____

c. Colossians 2:8_____

_____

_____

d. Jeremiah 14:14_____

_____

_____

e. Matthew 13:22-23_____

_____

_____

f. Jeremiah 23:16_____

_____

_____

7. What does the Lord say false prophets are
inwardly?_____

8. Look at Ezekiel 34:1-9. How are these false
prophets described?_____

_____

_____

_____

_____

_____

_____

_____

_____

_____

9. Why would false prophets resemble devouring
wolves? Who would their prey be?_____

_____

_____

_____

10. What are some biblical responses when we
suspect someone is a false prophet?

_____

_____

_____

11. What are some ways to determine if fruit from a tree is good or bad?_____

_____

_____

_____

12. What can we do to better our 'fruit-inspecting' skills when it comes to false prophets?_

_____

_____

_____

13. Fruit develops over time. What does this tell us about testing false prophets?_____

_____

_____

14. Being forewarned is being forearmed. How can the warnings in Matthew 7:15-20 help us in spiritual warfare?_____

_____

_____

_____

_____

---

2 Cor 11:13-15

For such are false apostles, deceitful workers, transforming themselves into apostles of Christ. And no wonder! For Satan himself transforms himself into an angel of light. Therefore, it is no great thing if his ministers also transform themselves into ministers of righteousness, whose end will be according to their works.

He Who Does

(Matthew 7:21-23)

In the last few verses we looked at false *prophets.* These teachings deal with false *followers.*

1. Who does Jesus say will enter into the kingdom of heaven according to Matthew 7:21?

_____

_____

2. What can someone say to the Lord thinking that will seal the deal to get into heaven?

_____

3. What should we see in someone who claims Jesus is their Lord?_____

_____

_____

4. What do we learn from Jesus about saying things that are not backed up by actions?

_____

_____

_____

_____

_____

5. Read Matthew 25:1-12. What is happening in this parable?_____

_____

_____

6. What works were the people taking confidence in according to Matthew 7:22?

_____

_____

_____

_____

7. What did the Lord say they were doing in Matthew 7:23?_____

_____

8. People can have religious fruit in their lives and still have sinful fruit concurringly. What do we learn about Jesus' concern for what comes out of our lives in these verses?_____

_____

_____

_____

_____

9. How can we avoid putting an emphasis on doing church activities and Christian ministries resulting in distracting or deceiving us from living lives pleasing to the Lord in other areas?

_____

_____

_____

_____

_____

_____

_____

10. What do these verses say about words and deeds?

    a. James 2:18-24_____

_____

_____

_____

    b. 1 John 1:6_____

_____

_____

    c. Luke 6:46_____

_____

_____

    d. Matthew 3:7-9_____

_____

_____

11. Whose name were these people using in Matthew 7:22?_____

12. How could being more cautious in whom we accept as fellow believers protect us when the storms of life come upon us?_____

_____

_____

_____

I Never Knew You

A Wise Man

(Matthew 7:24-29)

1. What word does this section of scripture start with?_____

2. Hearing and doing the things that the Lord has spoken in these 3 chapters is likened to something. What does Jesus liken this unto?

_____

_____

_____

_____

_____

3. What happens if we hear these sayings of Jesus and do not do them?_____

_____

_____

_____

_____

4. List some of the sayings of Jesus in Matthew 5-7 here that you believe you seek to put into practice?_____

_____

_____

_____

_____

_____

5. Which of the teachings in these three chapters do you find more challenging to you at this point of your life?_____

_____

_____

_____

_____

_____

6. Did both men in this parable of the storm-laden life face the same pressures?_____

7. What made the difference in how they weathered these conditions?_____

_____

_____

_____

_____

_____

8. What could we do to keep ourselves in check to be sure we don't slip into 'hearing' and not 'doing'?_____

_____

_____

_____

9. The infrastructure of our beings is directly related to the implementation of Jesus' words in these three chapters. How does knowing this help us be more attentive to these teachings?___

_____

_____

_____

_____

10. What do these verses teach us about the 'storms of life'?

    a. 1 Peter 1:6-7_____

    _____

    _____

    b. Acts 14:22_____

    _____

    _____

11. What does Jesus say the wise man's house was built upon?_____

12. What does Jesus say the foolish man built his house upon?_____

13. Contrast these two substances and how water impacts them._____

_____

_____

_____

_____

_____

_____

14. How did the people respond at the end of all these sayings and why?_____

_____
_____
_____

Lord. Thank You for these sayings. May I value them as building materials for my life. Awaken in me a great reverence for Your counsel.

- May my personality yield to Your precepts.
- May my will reflect Your Word.
- May my temperament reflect Your truth.

I trust that when I hear YOUR sayings and DO them I am storm-proofing my life for the inevitable floods, rain and winds that will beat upon my house. You are God. You are to be obeyed and my life is to be built using Your plumb line. I love You. Convict me of sin. Correct me when I am wrong. Lead me when I am lost. Redirect me when I take a wrong path. May my life show this world You are a Master Builder to the glory of Jesus Christ!

864-9 214-4333
203424

Made in the USA
Coppell, TX
08 September 2020

36276920R00059